LABOR OF LOVE

A Spiritual Companion
for Servant Leaders

JOE SCHROEDER

LABOR OF LOVE

A Spiritual Companion for Servant Leaders

Joe Schroeder

Copyright © 2017

All rights reserved.

Printed in the United States of America

DEDICATION

To Annie, my best friend and dear soulmate, who is the song in my heart and the spring in my step;

To my friends and family and to my brothers and sisters in education, who have inspired me daily and encouraged this work;

And most of all …

To the Almighty Lord, my Savior and Creator, who makes all things new and possible.

May this book support and renew all those who read it, especially those who serve His children so tirelessly and devotedly.

LABOR OF LOVE

FOREWORD BY DAMIAN LACROIX	7
INTRODUCTION: TENDING TO THE SPIRIT AND HEART OF THE LEADERSHIP JOURNEY	11
PART I: BECOMING MY BETTER, TRUER SELF	25
1: Service	26
2: Contentment and Faithfulness	30
3: Release	34
4: Patience	37
5: Surrender	41
6: Inspiration	46
7: Affirmation	50
PART II: ATTRIBUTES OF THE SERVANT LEADER	55
8: Eagerness	56
9: Vulnerability	60
10: Trust and Vigilance	65
11: Peacefulness	68
12: Courage	71

13: Fortitude   73

14: Humility   76

15: Unconditional Love   80

16: Radiance   85

PART III: SERVANT LEADERS IN ACTION   89

17: Harvesting What We Sow   90

18: Cultivating Relationships   93

19: Dealing with Trials   96

20: Seeking Tranquility   100

21: Pursuing Fellowship   104

22: Promoting Constructive Language   108

23: Being Joyful   111

24: Applying Discernment   114

25: Offering Forgiveness   118

26: Remaining Strong and True   123

BIBLIOGRAPHY   127

ABOUT THE AUTHOR   130

FOREWORD

I n a historically documented and famous public statement, Jesus said, "Come to me, all you who are weary and burdened, and I will give you rest. Take my yoke upon you and learn from me, for I am gentle and humble in heart, and you will find rest for your souls. For my yoke is easy and my burden is light."

Having devoted more than a quarter century in service to public education, I have witnessed an alarming escalation of the pace, complexity, and volume of the work over time. In routine conversations with K-12 educators, a common theme in their feedback is how overwhelmed they feel in their daily efforts to meet the diverse learning needs of their students. The ongoing challenge of trying to keep pace with relentless change is compounded by the fact that public education seemingly has become a punching bag for everything that ails our national psyche. For example, in his inaugural message on January 20, 2017, Donald Trump stated, "Americans want great schools for their children, safe neighborhoods for their families, and good jobs for themselves, but for too many of our citizens, a different reality exists ... an education system flush with cash but which leaves our young and beautiful students deprived of all knowledge."

Coupled with the stress of successfully adapting to individual learning needs within a dynamic global knowledge and information age, the net result of this persistent criticism is the typical educator feels breathless, bewildered, and beat down. Given this treatment, we should not be surprised that up to 50 percent leave the profession during the first five years (NCTAF Study)—and the number of college students who say they plan to major in education has reached its lowest point in 45 years (*The Chronicle of Higher Education*). Fickle state funding, skittish stakeholder support, and substandard salaries compound the difficulty of attracting and retaining the best and brightest to educate the 50 million children in our schools today. Sadly, one of our nation's most enduring and endearing institutions finds itself at an historic crossroads.

"Weary and burdened," many public educators long for a "rest" from the onslaught. In this book, award-winning educator, trainer, and coach Dr. Joe Schroeder offers a practical prescription for those who find themselves in this condition. Borrowing from the greatest educator of all time, Jesus Christ, Schroeder illuminates ancient biblical wisdom with refreshingly modern applications. As a longtime colleague and friend, I can attest to the transformation that I've observed in Joe's professional and personal life as he has "grown in the grace and knowledge" of *the* Master Teacher. Correspondingly, I am confident that the contents herein will illuminate a pathway to an easier yoke, and a lighter burden, as you pursue your labor of love.

Damian LaCroix
Superintendent
Howard-Suamico, Wisconsin

INTRODUCTION

Tending to the Spirit and Heart
of the Leadership Journey

Over 20 years ago, as I was beginning in my first principal role, my supervisor aptly described the administrator's job as "the world's greatest ongoing values-clarification exercise." And in a matter of a few weeks, I came to understand what he meant. Day in and day out, I had to make decisions that revealed, tested, and shaped my core values and—given my prominent role in the organization—also thereby revealed, tested, and shaped the core values of our school over time. As I embraced the challenges and opportunities at the leadership helm and got to understand myself better in the process, I also became ever more aware over time of my own shortcomings. For example, despite many dedicated efforts, I had to ultimately concede that I could not bring a resource to bear to *every* identified need; that I could not solve the problem every day for *everyone*; and many nights, I could not just flip a switch and turn off my mind from the daily flurry once my head finally hit the pillow. In fact, at some point, I had to come to terms with the additional stark realization that, in attempting to serve others so dutifully and completely, I had on far too many occasions provided little but token efforts to my greatest responsibilities and relationships outside of work—frankly, because I had little, if anything, left in the tank to give.

So 15 years ago, I pursued some specific means to address these concerns in my own life—some organizational and tactical approaches with my staff to become more efficient with our time, while also becoming much more effective in achieving the mission and goals of our most important work, both in school and outside of it. The significant gains organizationally and personally resulting from these efforts ultimately evolved into what today is the *Managing to Lead* workshops that I facilitate many times each year for my current employer, the Association of Wisconsin School Administrators (AWSA), located in Madison, Wisconsin. Through these workshops over the years, approximately 2,000 Wisconsin educators to date have explored the natural tensions between the workplace and our personal lives, with practical examples for raising the impact in both domains. But while these workshops have resulted in game-changing results for so many, they have also revealed to me their own limitations, as supports are needed for administrators on an ongoing basis. Moreover, time management and prioritization strategies that focus on the intellect and related thoughtful practices, though helpful, are not enough if we are to sufficiently support those who take on the responsibility of leading the organizations that nurture and develop our society's greatest treasure.

Given this background, then, the core problem as I see it is:

School administrators support the boundless needs of those they lead and serve. But who or what supports them—particularly in ways tending to the heart and spirit?

Said another way, where does one who continuously serves others replenish his/her personal leadership well—before the well goes dry?

As an educator now entering my 30th year in various roles of leadership, these nagging questions have been a constant in my life and are rooted in what I have come to view as a glaring void in the field of education—a profession focused almost entirely upon the *intellect* to the exclusion of the *spirit*, which is at the heart of all true and lasting leadership.

The deleterious effects of this fixation upon the intellect in educational leadership is described well by my dear friend and colleague, Damian LaCroix, in this book's Foreword. To his point, over my career, I have regularly observed many wonderful, deeply dedicated administrators struggle mightily under the burdensome yoke of servant leadership due to the lack of supports they are finding for their heart and spirit. In my view, these unfortunate cases of so many are further examples that sharpening the intellect alone cannot sufficiently replenish the servant leader's well over the course of the long and arduous journey.

This all raises an important question: if leadership is essentially an expedition of the spirit, then why aren't we talking more about it and equipping leaders with ways to better address and sustain the journey? The reasons, I suspect, are many but generally break down into either (1) that examination of the heart and soul understandably can be very personal and hence uncomfortable to discuss, and/or (2) such discussion can raise suspicion that someone (presumably like me, the author) is pushing a particular religious agenda.

Whatever the reason, to avoid discussing the importance of the heart and spirit to the leadership trek only contributes further to the ongoing void and silence on such critical matters in our field and in our lives—a silence that is <u>not</u> serving our children, our schools, our communities, our leaders, our families, or our nation well. **Furthermore, professional literature in education often ignores a key common component of high-impact servant leaders across time and place: that the leader's deep <u>outward impact</u> on his/her corner of the world is first made possible and sustainable by his/her <u>inward journey</u> of the heart and spirit.** Read any short stack of biographies on such leaders as Mahatma Gandhi, Nelson Mandela, Mother Teresa, Martin Luther King, Jr, or Abraham Lincoln and the link between the leader's inward exploration to his/her outward impact becomes abundantly clear. **And to be sure, for a society like ours in such great need of**

high-impact leadership, we ignore this *inward journey - outward impact link* **to our own peril!**

Therefore, to witness this dilemma and yet ignore the issue when I might be able to help it (leaving others to figure these critical mindsets and approaches out on their own over time, if ever) would, I believe, be a dereliction of my professional duty and my moral responsibility to support leaders in my chosen profession.

So, despite my initial apprehension, for these reasons and through gentle but persistent prodding of the Holy Spirit, I started blogging in November of 2014 under the simple title of "Labor of Love" as a means to help address this pervasive problem by sharing insights—mainly from Christian writings and beliefs—that have buttressed my spirit and heart, replenished my leadership well, and offered many practical approaches for sustaining my own leadership journey over the years. Ultimately, these blog posts over a period of over 2.5 years have culminated, through ongoing nudging of the Spirit and blog readers, into publication of this book, *Labor of Love: A Spiritual Companion for Servant Leaders.*

Okay, now you know some of the background responsible for the book before you. But you may have noticed that this book's subtitle is *A Spiritual Companion for Servant Leaders*, not necessarily just for education leaders. There is a reason for that. Like any author, I need to write from my own experiences. I am a person who possesses a deep-seated mission to **serve** in the field of public education. My experiences in this field have shown me a glaring problem and, through God's grace, also some helpful and productive means for addressing such a dilemma. But that said, you may be focused on serving humankind in an area/vocation outside of education OR just as part of your service to your fellow humans outside of any given vocation or work space whatsoever. Either way, in this book, I often use applications that speak directly to the educational leadership context, because that's what I know and can best offer. But I believe—and pray—that any reader viewing him/herself as a servant leader in any vocation or in any other aspect of life can see many areas of connection and support for his/her journey, as well, through the pages that follow. Feedback that I have received from many people outside of education who have read my *Labor of Love* blog posts over the past few years would attest to this resonance. So in short, while my personal mission to impact public education is the first and primary motivation for writing this book, I happily share this publication with a wider audience of anyone who considers himself/herself a servant leader. As I see it, servant leaders in virtually any aspect share common challenges. More important, through our common service to humankind, we are essentially all oaring the same boat, anyway.

Finally, the fact that the beliefs and resources I share in this book are drawn largely from a Christian perspective does nothing to diminish the fact that many servant leaders, perhaps like you, hold very different belief systems from mine (or perhaps may not even be very clear about what they truly believe at all). In acknowledging this reality, please allow me to be explicit about the following so that my intent is in no way misconstrued:

1) I appreciate and admire our pluralistic society.
2) I recognize that not everyone holds the same beliefs that I hold, and in no way is this book meant to assert my personal beliefs as those that everyone should hold.
3) I deeply believe in and support your ability to form your own personal beliefs and to hold to them as an unassailable human right.

That said, while I don't know what particular beliefs speak to your spirit and heart, I do believe it is essential to figure out what you do, in fact, believe and then to draw upon the resources of that belief system that tend to your heart and spirit, if the burdensome leadership journey is to be successfully managed—because the intellect by itself will not suffice. Once again, I write from what I know and believe. I humbly offer what God, through His amazing grace, has made clear to me, which countless times has been a tonic to my soul and a source of guidance and strength in my own leadership odyssey. I trust that what follows in this book will be a support to you in your adventure, as well. In fact, if you approach the contents of this publication with an open heart and mind, I am certain that a Higher Power will provide the strength and wisdom and support that you need.

This book is organized into three parts, each comprised of 7 to 10 reflections on various aspects of servant leadership (e.g., *inspiration* or *courage* or *humility*). The simple organization of a typical reflective segment begins with a provocative Bible verse and image, followed by discussion and application of some timeless concepts to present-day leadership, completed by a closing prayer. The reflective nature of each writing tied to scripture and prayer is intentionally designed to help readers build habits of introspection and prayerfulness that tend to development of the heart and spirit, as well as that of the mind. Moreover, the concise composition of each reflection allows either (1) for ease of targeted review and guidance responsive to a specific challenge that arises on a given day (for example, with one's need to be more *courageous*), or (2) as means for repeated review and contemplation of a specific aspect day after day in order to develop a particular "leadership muscle" of focus (for example, on becoming more humble) that ongoing attention and internal work will make manifest.

Part One starts by acknowledging that we are each gifted in unique ways. It doesn't matter who has which specific gift or in what quantity compared to someone else; what is important is that we can rightly discern our unique gifts and begin to build some means to make those fruits abundant and useful for the world. By establishing some personal foundations in key areas such as *patience, affirmation,* and *surrender,* we put ourselves on the path to becoming our better, truer selves.

Part Two then describes attributes of the servant leader. By reflecting on insights and supports from scripture, one can better learn what attributes to focus upon and make apparent. Some (like *humility,* *vulnerability,* and *unconditional love*) help the earnest leader maximize impact and a service orientation. Others (such as *courage, peacefulness,* and *fortitude*) acknowledge that the leader's path can be difficult and nearly overwhelming at times, but that there are timeless sources one can tap to allay fears, encourage the heart, and sustain the leadership journey.

Part Three focuses upon what faithful servant leaders do that are clear signs of their devotion and commitment to care for humankind. For example, this section explores how leaders deal with trials while sincerely cultivating relationships, offering forgiveness, and seeking tranquility. It is the leader's actions that are the best and truest signs of the state of his/her soul. So this section provides biblical resources, insights, and applications that can help the prospective servant leader tend to the internal work of the heart and spirit that can lead to deep impact in his/her corner of the world. Above all, Part Three acknowledges the fundamental truth that, in the final analysis, we each "harvest what we sow." Therefore, we must choose our actions and our path well.

All in all, it is such an incredibly humbling and, at times, unnerving thing to share one's innermost thoughts, shortcomings, and beliefs with the public at large. But throughout the entire process of developing my *Labor of Love* blog posts and writing this book, I have tried to be mindful of one of my favorite quotations from a cherished spiritual hero, Mother Teresa (now Saint Teresa) of Calcutta: **"I am a little pencil in the hand of a writing God who is sending a love letter to the world."** When I focus upon that simple image and give the inspiration and the writing up to the Spirit, I find that my anxieties and fears and unnecessary concerns dissipate—time and time again. Perhaps such an image can be similarly consoling and strengthening in your daily living, leading, and serving, too. You don't have to be *great*; you just need to be f*aithful*—and willing to earnestly serve as but a humble little pencil in the hand of a great and loving God.

In closing, I thank the Lord Almighty for providing His children with such a powerful and pervasive model of love that He has woven into the very fabric of the universe. I thank Him for the many years of my own leadership journey in the field of education that have revealed, shaped, and tested me in countless ways and which, through the crucible of these experiences, has provided me timeless and unforeseen lessons of love and service and fortitude. Most of all, I thank the Lord for planting in my heart the desire to join the countless others throughout all time and place who made a similar decision to serve as the simplest of instruments in His Almighty hand— in this universal and eternal labor of love. My friend, I pray that the Lord may use this book to strengthen your heart, mind, and spirit in immeasurable ways that can powerfully equip and sustain your own labor of love, too.

Joe Schroeder

July 2017

PART I

BECOMING MY
BETTER, TRUER SELF

1

SERVICE

"Each of you should use whatever gift you have received to serve others, as faithful stewards of God's grace in its various forms."

(1 Peter 4:10)

C hildren are often peppered with **"What do you want to be when you grow up?"** Looking back, a couple of the more amusing replies from a much younger version of me were "professional athlete" and "Broadway star." How about for you?

This simple, common question, reinforced in many different times and ways by our culture over the years, can cause many people later in life to erroneously and unwittingly conclude that *who* we are is tied to *what* occupation we do. For example, our culture would have me believe that who I am—my identity—is tightly coupled to whatever prestige or lack thereof comes with someone in my occupation, the social circles into which this identity allows me to congregate, the salary and perks that such a role commands, etc.

But our God makes us know that we each have inherent value, irrespective of our role in this world, because we are His children.

Truly, the question deserving of deep reflection for us adults, then, is <u>not</u> "what do you want to be?" or "what do you do?" but rather "who do you want to be?" And how can *what you do* create a better version of *who you can be*?

For example, if I want to be a better person in some way, there is great truth to the following paradox: **"We don't think ourselves into a new way of living. We live ourselves into a new way of thinking."** That is, applying myself in ways that manifest my God-given gifts to those around me allows me to become, over time, with God's grace, a better version of me—what Abraham

Lincoln referred to as "the better angels of our nature."

Of course, Christ—source for all real power—made this clear years ago to His disciples, who were jockeying for the "power position" at his right side. Christ's response, communicated humbly through word and deed, was that He "did not come to be served, but to serve." And that they should follow His lead.

So who are you, the real you underneath all the biographical information about race and gender and occupation and so forth? Who do you want to be? How could you find that better angel in your nature? Gandhi has some simple, yet powerful, advice that he also discovered through the opportunities and trials of his life: **"You will <u>find yourself by losing yourself in service</u> to your fellow man, your country, your God."** So you folks in servant leader roles, count your blessings! You already have a running start on discovering the real you underneath it all!

In my most hopeful hours, perhaps in a dream, I can imagine one day asking a young child the age-old question about what or who she wants to someday be. And instead of a normal response, I further envision that this young one, much wiser than her years, might instead reply, "When I grow up, I want to be a kind person, someone using my God-given gifts to deeply serve others."

So do I, dear one. So do I.

Dear Lord,

Thank you for the opportunity to serve Your Children, young and old. May I view service not only as my civic and Christian duty but more so as an ongoing opportunity to live myself into a new way of thinking—to increasingly walk in Your ways and, thus, become a better and truer version of Your creation in me. I pray that You plant in my heart a desire to pursue such a path forward and that You would always guide and encourage my steps along the way.

In Your name, I pray.

Amen.

2

CONTENTMENT AND FAITHFULNESS

"His master replied, 'Well done, good and faithful servant! You have been faithful with a few things; I will put you in charge of many things. Come and share your master's happiness!'"

(Matthew 25:21)

It's easy to be envious of others—or to be overly ambitious. Someone always seems to have things set up better. The grass is always greener on the other side. So it's very easy to fall into the mindset of the "constant comparative."

This situation arises in Matthew 25, from which the passage above is derived. In the story, before departing on a long journey, a master entrusts his wealth to three servants. The master gives one servant five bags of gold, another two bags of gold, and to a third servant, one bag. If you recall the parable, upon his return, the master discovered that the first two servants had each invested the treasure with much return—to his great pleasure. However, the master also discovered that the third had buried his treasure, with no impact for the time he had had it in his possession.

When I hear this story, it makes me wonder what the third servant must have been thinking. Seeing that his two co-workers were given much more treasure, did he become despondent or envious or even a bit spiteful upon his master's departure? Might such unproductive thoughts or feelings have contributed to him "burying his treasure?"

Thinking about our own lives, by falling into the trap of "the constant comparative," we can all find ourselves asking, "Shouldn't my lot in life be something bigger than this? Why don't I have what he/she has?" And if we are not careful, this mindset quickly can lead to despondency, envy, or spite. But it is very important for us to note that, regardless of the amount, EACH of the characters in the parable had SIGNIFICANT treasure in his possession. So do we! **It's not about how much**

you have; it's about what you do with what you have.

Our Lord has given us each abundant treasure (time, talent, energy, resources) to invest in this planet the few days and years we have been granted to make a difference. And let's be real. Regardless of the comparative degree of talent, treasure, or lot in life that we possess, the words of Mother Teresa apply: "We can do no great things. Only small things with great love."

Let us faithfully discharge the duties under our care, whether our assignment in life seems big or small, glamorous or mundane. Because faithfully pursued, our efforts WILL make all the difference for someone. In the words of Josh Shipp, "Every child is just one caring adult away from being a success story." So let us pursue our labor of love in the gift of the day before us.

Dear Lord,

Thank you for all the amazing gifts You provide. Let me not squander this treasure from Your generous hand, but rather use it to advance Your will in a world gravely in need of it. And understanding that no assignment in Your Almighty name is insignificant, let me always be thankful, content, and faithful to bloom wherever I am planted, for Your glory.

Amen.

3

RELEASE

"Finally, brothers, whatever is pure,
whatever is lovely, whatever is admirable—
if anything is excellent or praiseworthy—
think about such things."

(Philippians 4:8)

I t is easy to get caught up in the dealings of the
world, especially in those matters that tend to
be contentious or negative. Even though such
situations generally represent just a small
fraction of our day, we can easily dwell on these

above all others, stuck in some form of mental loop that plays over and over and over.

Surely, it is difficult to take charge of our minds, but this is what our Lord has asked us to do. And as this passage from Philippians asserts, a key means for doing this is to focus on the positive: the amazing creations of His mighty hand, the kind and loving act within the flurry of daily activity, the abundant blessings (large and small) that He reveals to us each and every day — if only we are aware and take notice.

We are called to be light to a dark world. But we are not to dwell on the darkness. When we fixate on the negative, we miss the opportunity to be agents of further good, while also sapping ourselves of some of the energy vital to making additional loving acts of kindness happen.

So deal justly with what comes your way. But then, with Your Maker's assistance, let it go, and focus on the positive. A little PMA (Positive Mental Attitude) can go a long way for you and for others, brightening up your corner of the world in the process.

Labor of Love

Dear Lord,

Thank you for the opportunity to serve Your children and minister to their needs. In the process of daily meeting my life's purpose, please be with me in guidance and comfort and wisdom. When I am anxious, please remind me to cast my burdens on You, and then move on in faith and trust and hope— knowing that, in You, the battle is already won, and the victory is already secure.

In Christ's name, I pray.

Amen.

4

PATIENCE

"... let us lay aside every weight, and the sin which so easily besets us, and let us run with patience the race that is set before us."
(Hebrews 12:1)

"Let's get movin'!" "Come on already!" "We don't have all day!" "Let's goooooo!"

My words—far too many times. The words of impatience.

Sometimes as a leader, I need to justifiably motivate others, create some urgency. So it's not that such language is inherently bad. And like many leaders, I consider myself a do-er. So the more we sit around and talk about things, the more it can feel like we are just letting time slip away. (We are burning daylight, people!!) But it is easy to have such words, and the indignant mindset that can often accompany them, become commonplace in daily living, crossing over quickly into frustration with others or with events or with myself because we are not working within MY timeline or MY agenda.

I get called up short on this whenever I reflect upon Galatians 5:22, where the Bible praises *patience* **as a fruit of the spirit**. In other words, if I truly am over time becoming more like my Maker through the work of the Holy Spirit, people should increasingly see me being the patient man I aspire to be, rather than the impatient one I have been or too often still am. But old habits die hard, even to the degree, ironically, that I can get impatient with myself about not becoming more patient!

This brings us to the passage above, where the word *patience* can initially seem an odd fit for someone who is running a race. That's because we often connote *patience* with some type of passive waiting or gentle tolerance. But in the above passage, the runner does not passively wait for slow-pokes or gently tolerate cheaters. No, a Christian runs the race by persevering through difficulties. **In the Bible, <u>patience</u> is <u>persevering</u> toward a goal, <u>enduring</u> trials, or expectantly waiting for a promise to be fulfilled. It's a very active, robust sort of patience.**

(https://gotquestions.org/Bible-patience.html)

And here's the heart of the matter. Oftentimes, the biggest barriers I face in my "race to the finish" are ones of my own making, with my own impatience as a major impediment—impatience which is often rooted (if I'm being totally honest with myself) in my own feelings of inadequacy, fear, or overwhelm in taking on the situation at hand. In these instances, I am not trusting that God will provide me all that is needed for HIS plan to work out perfectly within HIS timeline if I am simply willing enough to give up "control" of all of these concerns and place them in HIS hands, rather than in my own.

So the overall question for ongoing reflection: Can I lay aside all the obstacles and shortcomings that can distract and entangle me in my daily living so I can remain fixed on the final goal? In other words, **can I place my trust and patience in He who holds the keys to the eternal, knowing that, in the end—in God's hands and in God's time—all is well!**

Dear Lord,

Creator of all that is, thank You for Your boundless gifts, but particularly for the infinite patience and grace that You bestow upon me, though I come up short time and time again. May the patience You model help me to grow in patience with others and with myself. And may the patience that I aim to increasingly reveal to the world be the active, robust sort of patience which endures trials that arise, persevering to the very end, trusting that You have allotted sufficient time to accomplish ALL in Your plan, including whatever contributions You might have in store for me in the final resolution.

In Your Almighty and All-Loving Name, I pray and place my trust.

Amen.

5

SURRENDER

"Do not conform to the pattern of this world, but be transformed by the renewing of your mind. Then you will be able to test and approve what God's will is— His good, pleasing, and perfect will."

(Romans 12:2)

"L eave me alone! I'm fine. I've got this." Ever uttered such words? I suspect we all have. They are the words of the independent, self-reliant (even self-centered) person that the world would have us believe show that one has arrived as a full-firing adult.

But when you stop to think about it, there is lot of sub-text to statements like these. Like, *I have it **all** under **control***. In other words, *I need **nothin'** from **nobody***.

And then, as leaders in schools or in other walks of life, we get up to our armpits in issues and challenges so fast that, if we are being truly honest about things, this whole notion about being in control of everything (or even of anything!) becomes extremely laughable, extremely quickly.

There is tremendous grace in such overwhelming experiences, though. For were it not for moments like these, one could wallow in some misguided sense of self-sufficiency (***my*** *plan,* ***my*** *will,* ***my*** *world*) for a lifetime ...

In fact, it is exactly moments like these—times when we feel overwhelmed in our responsibilities and perhaps doubt why we ever thought we could do some good on this planet—when the words of James 4:7 ring especially true: "Submit yourselves, then, to God. Resist the devil, and he will flee from you."

In this short passage above, James gives us words to live by: submit yourselves to God, surrender to His will, His plan for you. Get your

head and heart around that and you will <u>truly</u> have what you need. Then you can <u>truly</u> say, "I'm fine."

So how do we get connected to His will, His plan?

Through prayer.

We see Christ doing this time and again in the Gospels, seeking the Father's counsel and His will, especially when times are tough. Through such actions, we observe Christ modeling for us what Paul describes in the passage at the top of this reflection: rejecting the world's patterns; seeking ongoing renewal of His mind and heart; testing and approving, through prayer, what God's will is—His good, pleasing, and perfect will.

In his classic, *With Open Hands*, Henri Nouwen tangibly describes this transition that we must make through prayer **from** the fallacy of *self-control* **to** a posture of *surrender* to Our Maker as the movement **from** clenched fists **to** open hands. We are often resistant to this transition (shown through our "clenched fists") because letting go of control does not "conform with the pattern of this world." Rather, it demands a relationship through prayer "in which you allow Someone other than yourself to enter into the very center of your person, to see there what you would rather leave in darkness, and to touch there what you would rather leave untouched." So we cling to what is familiar, even if we aren't proud of it. For it is easier to cling to a sorry past and/or an overwhelming present than to trust in a new future. In other words, because we fear that we might somehow lose ourselves (including the insecurities, problems, and hang-ups that make up some of our identity) along the way, we stand there with balled-up fists, closed to the Other who wants to heal us, to help us.

But if we can begin to open up our hands without fear, then the One who loves us can blow our sins away to make room for hope and peace in our lives, and to provide all-powerful support and guidance for the challenges in this world that loom before us. And when we do this, when we surrender to being His instrument, being a manifestation of His will on earth, we ultimately gain insights over time of His amazing benevolence and providence, more than we could ever deliver—or even imagine—for ourselves. Over time, we begin to understand that Our Lord responds to our prayers in one of three ways (and none of His answers are *no*, by the way).

Our Lord's responses to our prayers:

1) Yes

2) Maybe

3) I have a better plan!

Dear Lord,

I am so afraid to open my clenched fists! Who will I be when I have nothing left to hold on to? Who will I be when I stand before You with empty hands? Please help me to gradually open my hands and discover that I am not what I own, but what You want to give me—and what You want to give me is love—unconditional, everlasting love. Help me to trust that so You can lead me where You need me and I may revel in a deep and abiding relationship with You, the Maker of all that is and of all that is to be.

In Your Almighty Name, I pray and place my trust.

Amen.

6

INSPIRATION

"When the day of Pentecost had come, they were all together in one place. And suddenly a sound came from heaven like a rush of a mighty wind, and it filled the house where they were sitting. And there appeared to them tongues as of fire, distributed and resting on each of them. And they were all filled with the Holy Spirit and began to speak in other tongues, as the Spirit gave them utterance."

(Acts 2:1-4)

I n their classic of management literature, *Credibility: How Leaders Gain and Lose It, Why*

People Demand It, Kouzes and Posner cite three critical traits for developing leadership credibility: *honesty, competence,* and the *ability to inspire.* Of these three, the most daunting always seems to me to be the third—the ability to inspire others. That one seems to be the most outside my control. And just who am I to think I could influence or move someone else emotionally or spiritually, anyway?

When such fears and doubts arise, I often find myself coming back to this passage, which shows the arrival of the Holy Spirit to the apostles after Christ's death. Just like other leaders, the apostles had big work to do; they surely had their doubts; they knew there would be significant opposition along their journey. But they were not alone. Jesus had told them, "I will ask the Father, and He will give you another advocate to help you and be with you forever." (John 14:16).

And now we have this same advocate, the Holy Spirit, if we simply ask for His help.

But how do we best prepare ourselves to make the most of His assistance?

D.L. Moody, 19th century evangelist and founder of the Moody Bible Institute in Chicago, wrote one of the more convicting passages I have ever encountered regarding the process for being filled by the Spirit so that we can do inspiring work with and for others:

> *I firmly believe that the moment our hearts are emptied of selfishness and ambition and self-seeking and everything that is contrary to God's law, the Holy Spirit will come and fill every corner of our hearts; but if we are full of pride and conceit, ambition and self-seeking, pleasure and the world, there is no room for the Spirit of God. I also believe that many a man is praying to God to fill him, when he is full already with something else.* **Before we pray that God would fill us, I believe we ought to pray that He would empty us. There must be an emptying before there can be a filling;** *and when the heart is turned upside down, and everything that is contrary to God is turned out, then the Spirit will come ...*

It can be very disconcerting for leaders, so deep in our convictions, to let go of so much that we have clung to for so long. But Moody reminds us—exhorts us through his simple logic—to come to grips that letting go first is the only way. This is the pilgrim's journey. This is how we become His instrument. This is how we truly are filled with the stuff that moves men and women to levels of inspiration and action transcending human limits.

Therefore, Moody's conviction remains: **Can we empty ourselves of our own hang-ups and limitations so we can be filled with the boundless possibilities of the Almighty?**

That may be our biggest leadership and personal challenge of this day—and of every day!

Dear Lord,

Thank you for Your many gifts in my life. Among those, thank you for sending an Advocate, the Holy Spirit, to those who ask for His help. To this end, help me to empty myself of myself so I may be filled with Your Spirit and, in so doing, can fully play my part in serving, with others, Your children in ways that transcend human limitations, until that one day when we are all called home with You.

In Your name, I pray.

Amen.

7

AFFIRMATION

"I can do everything through Him
who gives me strength."

(Philippians 4:13)

D ecades ago, during my early days as an
aspiring teacher, a "tip" I frequently heard
from cagey veterans was, "Don't let your students
see you smile until Christmas." I took this as
hyperbole at the time, some sort of overstatement
by experienced hands trying to convey the
importance for a teacher to establish a well-
managed, orderly classroom environment. But

the frequency with which I heard this, even as overstatement, in my new profession helped me understand over time why so many students often felt turned off, rather than inspired, by school. It also made me wonder how in the world educators who held to such beliefs thought that they could somehow later "flip the switch" to create a lively and engaging setting for bringing out the best in their students when the stale classroom climate mold had already been cast months prior.

Of course, the switch almost assuredly never did flip, for this mantra comes from some deep place in the speaker, from a core belief in order and control, rather than in faith and trust, and a belief to such degree in the importance of control is hard to ever let go! To be sure, this mindset positions the teacher as the doler of knowledge and the sole source of order for the classroom domain through the power of the position, which unfortunately then leads to the energy of the classroom being too often used to maintain that position of power, rather than in the building up of others.

In contrast, high-impact educators hold a different belief. They understand that while an orderly classroom environment is certainly important, it must also be welcoming, inclusive, and nurturing. Rather than cling to power and control, high-impact educators take many efforts in the early days of the school year to *empower and partner with students* to create a strong environment for building up themselves and others. From its very genesis, this classroom climate is an orderly—but also an affirming— place. The high-impact educator holds the deep-seated belief that the building up of *knowledge* itself is never enough; it needs to be paired with the development of *confidence* so the learner can increasingly gain and share the fruits of learning and insight in a world greatly in need of them.

In many ways, this mindset of the high-impact educator seems aligned well with the above passage from Philippians: **"I can do everything through Him who gives me strength**." People working from this mindset embody—in both word and action—high expectations for self and others, conveying that effort matters and that the fruits of our efforts can be virtually limitless. **It's a very affirming stance to take, aimed at development and growth—an empowering stance that simultaneously helps ourselves and others connect to the real source of that power.**

Many of us have been products of a different mindset, though, where we may have been conditioned to focus on the negative in ourselves and in others. Through such negative messaging, we stifle potential and limit the original blessing that we have all received. Father Richard Rohr of the Center for Action and Contemplation provides some simple, practical, yet very powerful means to make the transition to a more affirming and growth-oriented mindset, an approach which turns such unproductive messages on their head:

> *Think of a negative phrase that you have said aloud or thought to yourself that stems from a sense of shame rather than from your inherent dignity. Turn it upside down and say, in first person, present tense, an affirmation of your God-given value. For example:*
>
> *I am unlovable ... I am infinitely loved.*
>
> *I don't have enough ... I have everything I need.*
>
> *I am stupid ... I have the mind of Christ.*
>
> *I am worthless ... I am precious in God's eyes, I am honored, and God loves me.*

Repeat the positive statement, aloud, slowly, with intention and trust, several times. **Then rest silently in the awareness that you are already**

and forever, without any effort or achievement on your part, a beloved child of God."

Dear Lord,

Thank You for the many gifts you provide. Among those gifts most cherished, thank You for making me precious in Your eyes, infinitely honored, infinitely loved. Help me to cultivate in myself and in others a deep and abiding peace that arises from the understanding that we are each a beloved child of God. And please let the power of today's passage settle deeply into my core so this belief *can guide my daily thoughts and actions: "I can do everything through Him who gives me strength."*

In Your Almighty Name, I pray,

Amen.

PART II

ATTRIBUTES OF THE
SERVANT LEADER

8

EAGERNESS

"Be shepherds of God's flock that is under your care,
watching over them—not because you must, but
because you are willing, as God wants you to be; not
pursuing dishonest gain, but eager to serve."

(1 Peter 5:2)

C an you remember a time when you were a
kid, perhaps biding your time on the
sideline, thinking, *Put me in, Coach. I'll show you
what I can do!* Or perhaps witnessing an older

sibling or neighbor have his/her "moment in the sun" and telling yourself, *Wait until I grow up and get MY chance!*

Well, you have it. Right now. Right where you are standing.

So how are you doing now that you finally have your shot?

In the game of life, each one of us—in one way or another—has been given a short opportunity to get out there and make a difference—to serve the needs of the greater team. No doubt you are *willing* to serve. But as the above passage implores, are you *eager* to serve? Do you possess that same ardent desire to get on the field and make a difference that you once did as a kid? Because now, your efforts don't just potentially influence the outcome of a contest, they may change the course of a life—or 20, or many, many more—including yours!

Now granted, it's easy for initial enthusiasm to wane. Matters become routine. Your particular role in this world might not match the grandiose hopes you once held for myself. Or perhaps it seems that your personal contributions somehow get lost—unrecognized even—amid all that is going on. Regardless, the eagerness we once possessed can easily go adrift, particularly if our reverie focuses on our "personal gain."

This passage reminds us to instead concentrate "on the flock under our care." Despite how large or small, how visible or invisible we might see our role, the Creator of All That Is has placed us *just where we are* at *precisely this point in time* to positively influence those with whom we daily interact and even those about whom we may not even be aware. Yet we know through faith that **our service is an integral part of the Master Game Plan, and <u>that</u> is an amazing thought to reflect and dwell upon, indeed!** And the Coach of All is calling your name right now to get on out there, to play out your role on the team and tend to His flock. So be enthusiastic and eager in your service, because you are part of something much bigger than any one of us could ever hope to accomplish alone. Bloom where you are planted.

Finally, while we should seek to continuously renew the eagerness of the inner child in each of us, we should pair that enthusiasm with the understanding of an adult—the right understanding—that none of this is about us or our personal glory, anyway. **All glory is His. All greatness is His. Simply expressed, our job is not to be great, but simply to be faithful ... to**

serve Him and His children "under our care" ...
to be the ultimate team player. To this end, we
might want to channel Mother Teresa, who
reminds us of the right heart and mindset to daily
bring forward in this regard: "**We** can do no great
things, only small things with great love."

Now get on out there, while the clock's still
ticking!

Dear Lord,

*Thank you for the opportunity to serve Your people, to
faithfully tend to the needs of the portion of Your flock
that You have assigned to me. I ask that You daily
renew in me not just the willingness to serve, but also
the eagerness to serve so that Your will be done and so
all my days may be filled with joy and impact until
that one day when You call me home and we eternally
celebrate the Victory that is already won.*

In Your Name, I pray.

Amen.

9

VULNERABILITY

"Though he was in the form of God, he did
not count equality with God a thing to be
grasped, but emptied himself, taking the
form of a servant, and being born
in human likeness."

(Philippians 2:6)

L ike many of my generation, *Bruce
Springsteen (aka "the Boss")* had a uniquely
formative influence, resonating in countless ways

and shaping how I view the human experience. A common figure in a typical Boss song is a tragic everyday "hero"—a sort of everyman down on his luck, who is torn between the tension of needing to present a tough face to the world, while underneath facing the reality of his own human shortcomings and seeing love as the only saving grace for a wandering soul on this cold, hard planet.

For example, in his iconic "Born to Run," the song's hero describes his plight as a "tramp ... out on the wire" who needs to "spring from cages" and the "death traps" that plague his place in this world. But despite the challenges of his predicament, the hero contends that "together we could break this trap," and **he makes both a bold <u>invitation</u> <u>and</u> an equally bold <u>admission</u>**:

> "Will you walk with me out on the wire?
> 'Cause I'm just a scared and lonely rider."

As leaders, how many of us are that honest? How many of us make ourselves that vulnerable, boldly admitting that we are also "scared and lonely," then pairing this divulgence with a bold invitation to come join us "out on the wire?"

Such naked honesty and vulnerability to this degree is not the norm. For example, in the world described in the "Born to Run" song," girls comb their hair in rearview mirrors and the boys try to look so hard." In our day to day of leading and living, there seems to be a similar preoccupation with appearance and projected toughness— being on top of one's game, being "in control." That's what we have come to expect from leadership. That's what leadership is, right?

But in the passage above from Philippians, Peter describes a radically different kind of leadership—in many ways as radically different today as it was 2,000 years ago. A leader in the form of Christ who empties himself, takes the form of a servant, makes himself vulnerable, and thus has his humanity arise.

These are hard concepts for a "scared and lonely" leader to come to. As Richard Rohr so succinctly explains, "We like control; God it seems likes vulnerability." Therefore, we often cling to the notion that leadership is about authority, control, and power over others, whereas **true leadership, as exemplified by Christ, is really about letting go, emptying ourselves of our selves so that we can be real with our people, take on the servant's stance, and watch our own humanity and community rise as a result.**

Thus, in the emptying of our pretenses, in the pairing of our bold admission alongside our bold invitation, we create conditions for a coming together and convey two powerful messages in the process: (A) courage is not the absence of fear but the overcoming of it, and (B) together, we have the strength to overcome anything we face.

So, will you walk with me out on the wire?

Dear Lord,

Thank You for the many ways that You guide my steps. Among those lessons, thank You for Your example of bold invitation and courageous vulnerability, a way of leading and living that changed the world! I pray that You will give me the courage and grace and humility to walk a similar path. In that fashion, help me to empty myself of my self, my ego, and my ambition, so I can be filled fully by the Holy Spirit in all that I do.

And in my daily leading and living, let me exemplify for others the refrain of Your classic hymn:

> *"Will you let me be your servant?*
> *Let me be as Christ to you*
> *Pray that I might have the grace*
> *To let you be my servant, too."*

Labor of Love

In the love of God, the peace of Christ, and the power of the Holy Spirit, I pray.

Amen.

10

TRUST AND VIGILANCE

"We put our trust in the Lord,
but we kept our powder dry."

-- Regimental Monument epitaph at Gettysburg
National Military Park

T here are over 1,300 monuments at Gettysburg National Military Park in Pennsylvania, befitting memorials to the over 50,000 casualties resulting from this most-critical moment of American history. While on a trip there years ago, I encountered one of the park's smaller memorials bearing an inscription that was *monumental* in stature. It's the passage noted above: "We put our trust in the Lord, but we kept our powder dry."

The wisdom and insight of this inscription is timeless. Certainly, as believers, we are to place our complete trust and faith in God, but not as mindless drones, scuffling along in life, waiting upon God to do both His part *and* ours. No, it's a much more active faith that is required. We are called to be agents of light and hope in a world daily battling darkness and despair. Fulfilling our role, we thus need to be ever alert and prepared to engage in the good fight, an effort that will likely require all that we have.

In short, **we have to get comfortable with the paradox of being fully *trusting* in our faith, while also being fully committed to *acting* on that faith. Or, said another way — <u>pray</u> as if it all depends on God; <u>act</u> as if it all depends on me.**

Dear Lord,

Thank You for calling me as one of Your own. Thank You for buttressing my faith. Help me to be attentive and vigilant to act on this faith, prepared to take on whatever the day brings.

Under Your triumphant banner, I cast my lot.

Amen.

11

PEACEFULNESS

"When the wheat sprouted and formed heads, then
the weeds also appeared."

(Matthew 13:26)

"Let us not be weary in doing good, for we will reap in
due season, if we don't give up."

(Galatians 6:9)

I n a classic segment from the sitcom *Seinfeld*,
Newman, the wacky letter carrier, works
himself into a lather explaining why so many
folks in his line of work *go postal*: "Because the
mail never stops. It just keeps coming and
coming and coming. And there's never a let up.

It's relentless! Every day it piles up MORE and MORE and MORE. And you GOTTA get it out! But the more you get it out, the more it KEEPS COMING IN!! ..."

People serving others can get similarly overwhelmed to the breaking point at times. Day after day, we toil in dedicated efforts to improve the human condition. But, drawing from the passage of Matthew above, as we survey the fruits of our labor, we can at times feel defeated that somehow new "weeds" have sprouted out amidst the "wheat" that we have been trying to cultivate. The "weeds" just KEEP COMING IN!! Somehow, despite our best efforts, every day brings MORE and MORE and MORE to tend to!

It is times like these when I have been heartened by the counsel of Galatians 6:9: "Let us not be weary in doing good, for we will reap in due season, if we don't give up."

And key to not "being weary" is to accept that **it is our job to simply do good work the best that we can discern it and then leave the rest up to God.** That means we don't spend time separating out the wheat from the weeds, trying to sort out the "good guys" from the "bad guys," or figuring out the tally. No, we just do our part and leave all the rest, including the ultimate reaping, up to Him. **That is the pathway toward peacefulness.**

Yes, we clearly live in a fallen world. But thankfully, Christian maturity provides the ability to live joyfully in such a place—with all its imperfections. So do your work faithfully—and let the rest go. In so doing, you will be pursuing the pathway of peacefulness, walking in step to the words of the old standard: "Let there be peace on Earth, and let it begin with me ..."

Dear Lord,

Thank You for allowing me to be an instrument in Your Mighty Hand. Help me to trust that, amidst my toil, no work done in Your name or for Your purposes is ever inconsequential. I look forward to the grand harvest that YOU will one day gather. In the meantime, grant me Your peace, which surpasses all understanding, to guard my heart and my mind in Christ Jesus.

Amen.

12

COURAGE

"You were made ... for just such a time as this."

(Esther 4:14)

"That's just not right! What's the world coming to these days? *Someone* should do *something* about *that*!"

This passage from Esther reminds us how our location and position in the world is no coincidence. The Lord has a plan for each of us and has gifted us in unique ways to carry that plan out. But ultimately, it depends on us to act—

to let our conscience be our guide and act on the courage of our convictions.

Yes, the world has a load of problems—and then some. And whether the deepest of the world's problems can fully be "solved" is a topic for further discussion. But there is no question that leadership can change the color of any situation and that the "someone" who should do "something" about "that" is likely you.

So listen to that "still small voice," build up your resolve, and dive into the situation at hand, remembering that God doesn't call the prepared; He prepares the called. Trust that and believe in that –for you were made for just such a time as this...

Dear Lord,

Thank You for creating me with Your grand designs in mind. Please help me to discern my place and my purpose in this world. Then may I act courageously, knowing that with You I am never alone.

For Your glory,

Amen.

13

FORTITUDE

"Behold, I have made your face strong against their faces, and your forehead strong against their foreheads. Like adamant stone, harder than flint, I have made your forehead; do not be afraid of them, nor be dismayed by their looks, though they are a rebellious house."

(Ezekiel 3:8-9)

There is a lot of anger in this world. Some of it warranted, much of it not. But if you are a leader of any sort, you will be dealing with it.

Some of it will find you simply because you are the face of the group. Other times, it will be a product of setting some reasonable boundaries for folks who aren't used to them—at least for themselves. Or it will occur because the unlimited desires of others collide with a world of limited resources. And hard choices have to be made. Still, on other occasions, anger flares up for … who knows what reason! But people are upset, determined to let the whole world know, and someone's head is going to roll. Growl! Hiss! Roarrrrrrr!

And typically the most painful of these situations occurs when the anger, the ganging up, perhaps even the betrayal comes from within the group— the very folks who you are trying to responsibly lead and serve.

In such situations, I have found this passage from Ezekiel to be of comfort—not because I aspire to be some hard-headed jerk. On the contrary, seeking to understand before being understood, meeting legitimate needs in full whenever possible, finding win-win—all of these should be hallmarks of the servant leader. But there are, regrettably, times when such everyday approaches no longer serve the situation at hand—when, after due discussion and deliberation, it's time to articulate a position, demonstrate fortitude, and endure whatever is to follow.

It is important in difficult moments like these to recall that you are not alone. Our Lord is the rock who can fortify you with the strongest of His stone. If needed, He can match any force brought up against you with equal force—and then some. For geology simply expressed is "time + pressure." And in God, you have the power of eternity on your side of the equation.

Dear Lord,

Thank You for the opportunity to lead and serve Your children. Help me to daily be an instrument of Your peace. Strengthen me for the burden of each day; fortify me for whatever comes my way.

On the rock of Your truth and love, I will stand, endure, and thrive.

Amen.

14

HUMILITY

"Humble yourselves, therefore, under God's mighty hand, that He may lift you up in due time."

(1 Peter 5:6)

We live in a culture that glorifies, and sometimes seemingly deifies, the individual. Athletes, musicians, celebrities, politicians are made larger than life, often getting caught up in and promoting their own narrative, the hype about them and their greatness. *I have arrived. I am the greatest! Pay me homage, World. Show me the money!* Then months or years later, we are not surprised to witness the other end of the same narrative, the crash and burn that all too often follows—as "pride comes before a fall."

But amid this cult of personality, I am regularly encouraged by images, like this one, which convey that some very gifted people take cues for their conduct and daily walk from Christ, who said, "Take my yoke upon you and learn from Me, because I am gentle and humble in heart ..." (Matthew 11:29). So while the world may heap praise on them, such "celebrities" go counter-culture: applying their God-given gifts to the situation at hand earnestly and humbly, as Christ modeled through his ministry, to give immediate credit and praise where it is rightly deserved—to the Source of all gifts.

For folks like us in less conspicuous walks of life, it might be important to remember that being humble does not mean that someone has a poor self-concept; it's just that he/she is not self-centered. For as C.S. Lewis so rightly pointed out, **"Humility is not thinking less of yourself but of thinking of yourself less."** Such an orientation bodes well for leaders, as is made evident by John Wooden, perhaps "the greatest" coach of all time in any sport, who led the UCLA men's basketball program to 10 national championships in 12 years, including an unprecedented 7 in a row. But Wooden humbly commented about all these accomplishments, "It's amazing how much can be accomplished if no one cares who gets the credit." That said, it is important to note that Coach Wooden was no shrinking violet. He expected his players to be aggressive; specifically, he expected that, if errors were to occur, they should be "errors of *commission*, rather than ones of *omission.*" In other words, while we are not to be arrogant or reckless in application of our gifts, we should apply them with great vigor of heart and soul.

In his classic book of management literature, *Good to Great: Why Some Companies Make the Leap ... And Others Don't,* Jim Collins found that a key reason for the rare organization of excellence was that it was led by a Level 5 leader, <u>a person who builds enduring greatness through a paradoxical combination of personal humility plus professional will.</u> It took years of dedicated research for Collins to arrive at this important finding. But Christ had already modeled this powerful combination of deep will with personal humility over 2,000 years ago, and it's what He wants from us.

So how well are you living your gifts with great confidence and vigor, yet with deep humility and gratitude? It's what Jesus would do...

Dear Lord,

Thank You for bestowing on me Your gifts, both great and small, that align with Your grand purposes. Help me to know my gifts and to share them freely in ways that bring light to this world. May You always strengthen and guide me to share these boldly yet humbly—and always with great thanks!

In Your name, I pray.

Amen.

15

UNCONDITIONAL LOVE

"If it is possible, as far as it depends on you, live at peace with everyone. Do not take revenge, my dear friends, but leave room for God's wrath, for it is written: 'It is mine to avenge; I will repay,' says the Lord ... Do not be overcome by evil, but overcome evil with good."

(Romans 12:18-21)

W e seem to possess a very superficial and even flippant regard for the word *love* in our society:

"I love pizza."

"Don't you just love it when she says things like that?"

"They have been dating for six months now. It must be love!"

Perhaps because of this, we will occasionally hear people distinguish these types of "love" from *unconditional love,* **which means that I care about the happiness of another person irrespective of his/her behaviors and without any thought for what might be in it for me**. Of course, the classic example of this is God's love for humankind.

I bring this up because so many of us strive to serve others—to function as servant leaders. But to possess a **true** heart of service seems to require that I care about the happiness of another person without any thought for what might be in it for me. In other words, to possess a true heart of service entails that I harbor unconditional love for all those around me. That can be a hard row to hoe for many reasons. Chief among them is that some people present themselves in ways that make them very hard to love! And, as any leader likely has experienced, some of these folks you serve may even seem to view you—for whatever reason—as their sworn enemy and are seemingly on a mission to damage and destroy you in any fashion that they can.

Mother Teresa and her Missionaries of Charity knew well the challenges of daily bearing a heart of unconditional love to the world with all its warts, rough edges, and hostility. The words below, sometimes referred to as "Do It Anyway," are generally attributed to Mother Teresa. As was true for her and for us, they beautifully articulate the challenges of daily serving <u>all</u> those who we encounter, unconditionally, in ways consistent with how Romans 12 calls us to lead our lives.

"People are often unreasonable, irrational,
and self-centered.
Forgive them anyway.

If you are kind, people may accuse you of
selfish, ulterior motives.
Be kind anyway.

If you are successful, you will win some
unfaithful friends and some genuine enemies.
Succeed anyway.

If you are honest and sincere,
people may deceive you.
Be honest and sincere anyway.

What you spend years creating, others could
destroy overnight.
Create anyway.

If you find serenity and happiness,
some may be jealous.
Be happy anyway.

The good you do today will often be forgotten.
Do good anyway.

Give the best you have,
and it will never be enough.
Give your best anyway.

In the final analysis, it is between you and God.
It was never between you and them anyway."

In closing and in a similar vein, iconic musician Stevie Wonder—physically blind but possessing a vision for how to justly live that far exceeds most of us—often bids farewell to his audiences through a convicting message: "**Use your heart to love somebody. And _if_ it is _big_ enough, use your heart to love _everybody_!**" This is big work, indeed, especially if we are to love everyone, unconditionally!! But this is our calling. This is our charge. This is how we are to serve. Romans 12 makes this abundantly clear.

Labor of Love

Dear Lord,

Thank You for the opportunity to serve my Brothers and Sisters in all their forms around me. Please help me to acknowledge that, in the role of servant leader, You have provided me a positional hammer that I can use either as a tool to build people up or as a device to tear them down. How I use that tool is up to me, but Your blueprint for me is clear. May You always tend to my heart, enlarging its capacity to daily live the unconditional love that You model so amazingly for me and for all of Your creation.

In Christ's name, I pray.

Amen.

16

RADIANCE

Mike Ford, Better Together Photography

"Neither do people light a lamp and put it under a
basket. Instead they put it on its stand, and it gives
light to everyone in the house. In the same way, let
your light shine before others, that they may see your
good deeds and glorify your Father in heaven."

(Matthew 5:15-16)

I t's easy—even popular—to be a cynic these
days. Pick a side on the ongoing debate,

furrow your brow, unload your opinions, point your finger vigorously, and jump into the fray. You will find many like-minded friends.

It's harder—often unpopular—to be an optimist. Attempt to inject some understanding, compassion, or hope into the argument and see how quickly you can be written off as naive, misguided, or "not one of us!" Therefore, even if we harbor such a perspective, given the current social and political climate, our protective instincts may have us hold such views close to the vest or, as the Matthew passage describes, "under a basket." It's just easier that way.

But that's not the way we are to live. We need to be children of light, and we are called to share this light with the world around us.

And our foundation of faith in Christ is reason for both (A) our uncommon view on matters and (B) strength for confidently living that viewpoint out in society at large.

For rooted in God, we can be at peace with the paradoxes and shortcomings of this world and largely immune to the crowd thinking and its false promises. In so doing, we can let go of the fear that might otherwise obscure our light—a concept not only expounded in the passage above from Matthew, but also by Nelson Mandela in his 1994 inauguration speech upon assuming the presidency of South Africa:

Our deepest fear is not that we are inadequate.

*Our deepest fear is that we are
powerful beyond measure.*

*It is our Light, not our Darkness,
that most frightens us.*

*We ask ourselves, who am I to be brilliant, gorgeous,
talented, fabulous?*

*Actually, who are you NOT to be?
You are a child of God.*

Your playing small does not serve the World.

*There is nothing enlightening about shrinking so that
other people won't feel unsure around you.*

*We were born to make manifest the glory of God
that is within us.*

It is not just in some of us; it is in everyone.

*As we let our own Light shine, we unconsciously
give other people permission to do the same.*

*As we are liberated from our own fear, our presence
automatically liberates others.*

So trust, believe, make manifest the glory of God within you and be heartened by the way your simple witness and daily living, over time, lifts up others. Let your light shine!

Dear Lord,

Being an optimist in this world is not easy. But as Christians living out our beliefs, we really have no other choice. So let us continually live out our faith vigorously, thereby giving testament through our daily words and actions and radiance that, in Christ, the battle is already won and the victory is already assured.

In Your Almighty name, we pray.

Amen.

PART III

SERVANT LEADERS
IN ACTION

17

HARVESTING WHAT WE SOW

"The harvest is plentiful, but the workers are few. Ask
the Lord of the harvest, therefore, to send out
workers into His harvest field."

(Luke 10:2)

A new school year ushers in a new season —
a season of sowing, of cultivating, and,
ultimately, of harvesting — a season of
anticipation, preparation, enthusiasm, and
trepidation all tied into one. For in line with the

above passage, there is so much good work to do with the hearts and minds of our youth and those who serve them. There are so many who can profoundly benefit from our daily toil in our field—the field of education. How exciting to be rooted in a vocation that has so much impact on His seed!

Yet, as the passage also conveys, the work before us exceeds the reach of any one person, or even one profession. A prospect such as this can be daunting, even intimidating—even more so when one considers what Christ says a bit later in Luke 10, "Go! I am sending you out like lambs among wolves." In all of our well-intended service and optimism, we are reminded that our mindset and commitment to others is not universally shared. Therefore, we need to "gird up our loins," for the school year ahead will surely incur conflict and challenge and strife. Yet we pick up the tools of our trade and head out to the fields with determination because that is where the harvest lies, that is where we are called to serve.

But more than anything, in this school year fraught with emotions ranging from enthusiasm to anticipation to trepidation, **we should especially take heart from the fundamental law**

of the harvest, which is concisely expounded in Galatians 6:7-8: "Whatever a man sows, this he will also reap. For the one who sows to his own flesh shall from the flesh reap corruption, but the one who sows to the Spirit shall from the Spirit reap eternal life."

Dear Lord,

Thank You for the sublime honor of tilling Your fields, of serving Your creation. Let any anxiety about the school year dissipate in the knowledge and confidence that You always go before us and are always with us. Sow in our own hearts the good seed that we can then distribute and make fruitful ten and twenty fold in that portion of Your garden which You have entrusted to our care. In all things, help us to be good and faithful servants to our sisters and brothers, Your children, until that one day when You finally call us home.

In Your name, we pray.

Amen.

18

CULTIVATING
RELATIONSHIPS

"But now faith, hope, love abide, these three;
but the greatest of these is love."

(1 Corinthians 13:13)

We are living in a results culture. That certainly is the case for those working in education these days. Quarterly reports, progress monitoring, collective accountability, levels of performance, effectiveness scores—these are but a few of the means aimed at holding educators responsible for moving the needle on student achievement and success.

But Dave Weber, educational consultant and speaker, effectively makes the case why we should start with cultivating robust staff relationships and school community if we truly are dedicated to transforming learning results for students. In his arguments, Dave points to the research of Dr. Roland Barth, who found that "the nature of the relationships of the adults that inhabit a school has more to do with the school's quality and character and with the accomplishments of its pupils than any other factor." Similarly, the Harvard Principals' Center asserted that "the most powerful predictor of student achievement is the quality of the relationships among the staff."

In a results culture focused on *hard data*, these reminders about the *soft skills* of relationship and community building are helpful and timely reminders. But for Christians, these findings should not be all that surprising. Two thousand years ago, Jesus asserted that **all the Law and the Prophets could be summed up in just two commandments: (1) love God and (2) love your neighbor (Matthew 22:36-40). Therefore, ultimately everything in life comes down to our**

relationship with our Maker and our relationships with people. And in both, we are to display love.

Maybe the Beatles had it right when they attested that "All You Need is Love." At least, it seems, that's where we should start and sustain the focus. In an accountability culture on steroids, keeping the focus on love and relationship is arguably more important now than ever.

Dear Lord,

Thank You for showing me what true love is. Help me to crave an ever deeper relationship with You, so that You can teach me Your ways. In my daily walk, teach me how to not only talk like a Christian, but, more important, how to love like Christ through my relationships with those whom I lead and serve—so people may know that I am a Christian by my love.

Into Your warm embrace I commend my spirit.

Amen.

19

DEALING WITH TRIALS

"I am the true vine, and My Father is the vinedresser. Every branch in Me that does not bear fruit, He takes away; and every branch that bears fruit He prunes, that it may bear more fruit."

(John 15:1-2)

A s Christians, we are expected to positively impact others, leave things better than we found them, make a difference. Or, as expressed through the common metaphor of scripture, we are to show ourselves to be "fruitful"—"for a tree is known by its fruit" (Matthew 12:33).

Okay, that concept makes sense. Make a difference. Be fruitful. Got it.

But in order to make a difference, we actually have to daily wade into the world, with all its problems and schemes. In order to positively impact others, we need to engage in their affairs, dysfunctional as they may often be. In order to leave things better than we found them, we regularly have to deeply invest of ourselves, for token efforts simply won't do. But in deep investment, we expose ourselves in ways that, frankly, may leave marks. In working to change things, improve conditions, and help others, the world is likely to push back—and often with a vengeance! Forces collide, claws come out, and for all our well-intended efforts, we can feel bruised, battered, crestfallen, or even indignant in the process.

In such times, we may feel tempted to bemoan our own sufferings and trials. *I was only trying to help. So why does it now seem like I'm the one suffering? That's not fair.*

But today's scripture from John reminds us that doing good for others, despite personal suffering, is the way of the Christian. It was the choice Christ made for us, as well. Christ is the vine, and we are the branches. Like branches from the vine, our fruitfulness comes from our source. **In efforts to expand the fruitful influence of our lives on others, we should expect numerous trials and personal sufferings (i.e., pruning) along the way. It's the way of God's vineyard. Through such pruning, we are cut back again and again, essentially recreated over time into a better form of ourselves—one more befitting of the fruitful vine from where we originate.**

So the next time you feel like complaining because of some burden faced in helping others, remind yourself that this is a signal that you, a faithful servant, are being pruned—so that you may grow through suffering to make even more of a difference, be even more fruitful, for a world in dire need of it.

Dear Lord,

Thank You for placing me in Your vineyard. Make me fruitful. Thank You for the loving hand that You bring to my growth and development. Help me to understand and accept your regular pruning that makes me more pleasing to Your eye and more fruitful to the harvest in Your vineyard.

Into Your Almighty and loving hands, I place my faith and trust.

Amen.

20

SEEKING TRANQUILITY

"Do not be anxious about anything, but in everything, by prayer and petition, with thanksgiving, present your requests to God. And the peace of God, which transcends all understanding, will guard your hearts and your minds in Christ Jesus."

(Philippians 4:6-7)

D o you know someone who seems to never be rattled? The sky may be falling in one way or another, yet he/she is as cool as a cucumber? Damian, a dear friend and brother in my life, is like this. When asked about it, Damian heads to this passage as foundational to his perspective.

In this verse, the apostle Paul is not mincing words. In fact, he writes in the form of a command: "Do not be anxious about anything" because to do so is to sin. To do so is to fail to trust that God is big enough to handle it.

Sometimes that's easier said than done. Many of us, in our work and daily living, encounter some absolutely terrible, even horrific, things. Read the paper, watch the news, scan social media, reflect on a "bad week" and all sorts of examples and images will come readily to mind. Clearly, we live in a broken world, where the flaws of man can impinge upon our daily walk and cast our faith asunder if we are not vigilant.

In moments like these, a discipline that people like Damian enlist is to come back to this passage for strength and guidance—and for "the peace of God, which transcends all understanding." Graced with such peace through prayer, we can then move off of the anxiety-riddled concept that we can somehow figure out, take on, and solve all the world's problems to simply discern, "**How**

can I serve here ... in this place ... as an agent of
light ... today?"

With such discipline over time to cast my
concerns upon God through prayer, then free my
mind to trust and serve humbly as His
instrument, I allow myself to embrace—and even
enjoy—whatever comes my way, in the only
lifetime that I will ever have. Over time, through
such disciplines and through God's grace that
comes from them, **my hope is to one day receive
a gift provided to the mature Christian: the
ability to live joyfully and without worry in a
broken world.**

Dear Lord,

*I recall the words of the classic hymn: "Oh, what peace
we often forfeit; Oh, what needless pain we bear; All
because we do not carry everything to God in prayer
..." So today I cast my concerns at Your feet. May I
build the discipline to regularly bring my concerns
through prayer and petition, with thanksgiving, to
You. Help me to let any anxiety go and seek Your
tranquility, knowing that, though the waters may
rage, I will one day claim my eternal safe harbor in
You.*

In the peace of Christ, I pray.

Amen.

21

PURSUING FELLOWSHIP

"As iron sharpens iron,
so one man sharpens another."

(Proverbs 27:17)

T oo often, we go it alone. Usually when that happens, we suffer, as the forces of the world smash up against us day after day. Naturally, facing such fury alone, we weaken. And if we take the solitary path too long, we risk being overwhelmed by bitterness, indecision, depression, or fear, ultimately swamping down our progress to some sort of near paralysis. As

U2's Bono exhorts a friend who, in one of the band's more famous ballads, goes it alone: "You've got stuck in a moment, and now you can't get out of it."

Leaders, in particular, if not careful, can regularly fall into such a trap. Sometimes this is due to the nature of the position, other times due to the press of issues before us, and in other instances, simply because we don't know where to start in explaining our situation to another.

But God made it clear from the beginning that it is not good for man to be alone. So He has given us the gift of one another. Through the analogy of the passage above, just as there is mutual benefit in rubbing two iron blades together, so is there means forward in fellowship with one another, particularly in fellowship that is sharpened by interaction around the word of God. For wherever two or more are gathered in His name, He is there, too, adding His grace and blessing to the equation.

This approach was reinforced when several family members and I viewed the Oscar-nominated picture *Selma*. This movie provided insight into the personal challenges that Dr. Martin Luther King, Jr. faced in addressing major wrongs of our society. On several occasions in the film, we see MLK at a near breaking point, as he feels the full force of the world in all its ugliness press upon him as the figurehead of the Civil Rights Movement. But in each of these moments, he intentionally takes measures to NOT go it alone, but rather, to seek fellowship. In one scene, he makes a late-night call to a friend, asking her to sing him a soothing gospel to tend to his fearful soul. In another, he gains strength through the rock hard support of his wife, despite his waywardness. In another, through the good counsel and timely reminder of a relevant biblical passage from a trusted friend, MLK becomes emboldened to persevere through his fear to committed action for the greater cause. And always, by turning to prayer, he finds guidance, strength, and support. Now, if someone of MLK's stature didn't go it alone, why should you?

Without a doubt, Martin Luther King, Jr. was a tremendous leader, speaker, and human being — arguably one of the greatest of all time. But *Selma* helped me to draw this conclusion for consideration: **MLK's <u>discipline to seek fellowship amidst trial</u> was perhaps his greatest strength, and perhaps the primary reason for his lasting legacy today. And that's a discipline that any of us can choose to develop.** Now, given such regular "sharpening" through fellowship, just imagine how effective of an instrument that you might be in Your Maker's hands!

Dear Lord,

I thank You that I need not go it alone. Please help me to always remember that and to build into my life the disciplines of Christian fellowship, prayer, and interaction with Your word. Strengthen me for the path ahead. Sharpen me in Your word. Make me an instrument of Your peace.

Amen.

22

PROMOTING CONSTRUCTIVE LANGUAGE

"Let no corrupting talk come out of your mouths, but only such as is good for building up, as fits the occasion, that it may give grace to those who hear."

(Ephesians 4:29)

As a kid, I recall adults regularly instructing us, "If you have nothing good to say, say nothing at all." It was a simple message, easy to understand, that spoke to the conscience and reminded us to give others the benefit of the doubt, to treat others with care, and not to judge. Heaven knows that we were not perfect in those days by any means (and, frankly, often received these words as a correction when we had somehow stepped over the line). But I remember this message having an impact, on both me and on the environment where I was trying to find my way.

These days, I wonder how often any of us hear such wise counsel. More to the point, I wonder how often we share it and model it in our daily walk, now that <u>we</u> are the adults. And, man, talk about a world in need of it—a world growing daily in hot-faced rhetoric, finger-pointing, division, fear, and violence.

To be sure, at times, it is very difficult to show restraint in our actions and in our speech; it's hard to reveal a maturing heart to the world. Meanwhile, it seems rather easy, even expected these days, to jump into the war of words and weigh in on umpteen issues that color our world. But, in line with this passage, **are our words constructive—seeking solutions that bring God's children together—or are they just contributing to the growing divide, the intensifying din?**

Before we utter another word, we would be wise to recall Christ's reminder that it's not what we take in and consume (from what we may perceive as a highly flawed world) that degrades us, but rather what comes out of our own mouths—as "the things that come out of the mouth come from the heart, and these defile a man." (Matthew 15:18).

So judge not, lest ye be judged (Matthew 7:1). Moreover, choose our words and tend to the state of our own heart well, so we are not contributing to the very problems we are trying to solve.

Dear Lord,

In a world full of sound and fury, remind me to seek quiet moments in each day so that I may hear Your voice, so that I might benefit from Your edifying counsel. Make me an instrument of Your peace through both my words and deeds, that my daily walk may build up all of Your children and give grace to those in my sphere.

Amen.

23

BEING JOYFUL

"Consider it pure joy, my brothers and sisters,
whenever you face trials of many kinds,
because you know that the testing of
your faith produces perseverance.
Let perseverance finish its work so that you may be
mature and complete, not lacking in anything."

(James 1, 1:2-4)

I t's very easy to be a grump these days. Hard-
line rhetoric and "us-them" positioning seems
to rule the day, as if that is what advanced living
and thinking is. Our world—even our little

corner of it—seems unceasingly and increasingly locked in the sort of conflict that revels in problem-finding more than in solution-seeking, putting people in boxes that magnify division more than inform a dialogue. Contributing to all this is an environment that far too often lacks even the most basic level of human civility and common decency. Yes, it's very easy—and popular—to be a grump these days.

But, as this passage from James 1 reminds us, we are called to be joyful, even (and especially) in the face of trials such as these. In fact, we are to *joyfully persevere*. So let us choose to set a more productive tone. Let us discern how we can serve in this place and with the people in front of us, then do so joyfully and even jovially. In so doing, we persevere in the steps of our Savior, knowing that the ability to live joyfully in a flawed world is a mark of Christian maturity.

More than anything, though, **let us choose to not be just another group of grumps who fail to reveal through word, action, and disposition the truth of our Almighty God and His joy and peace beyond comprehension.**

We set the tone. We have a responsibility to be points of light for a world in desperate need of it. So let us choose to be visible reminders to those around us that, in Christ, the battle is already won, the victory is already secure. Let us choose to go out today to live, persevere, and grow—WITH others, in joy.

Dear Lord,

Thank you for the gift of this day. Help me to embrace and enjoy whatever comes my way, viewing it as a sacred treasure. Strengthen me so that I may persevere through whatever trials I might face to always be a reflection of Your joy and peace beyond comprehension.

In Your name, I pray.

Amen.

24

APPLYING DISCERNMENT

"Admonish the idle, encourage the fainthearted, help the weak, be patient with them all."

(1 Thessalonians 5:14)

How do I justly lead others when their needs, dispositions, and motives are often so very different? If you are like me, you may have sought out assistance by reading untold numbers of books, pursued numerous conversations on the subject, tried to learn from various real-life situations over the years, etc. In all those efforts, I have found that one of the most insightful of all sources is packaged in a simple, one-sentence recommendation from the apostle Paul to a start-up church in Greece nearly 2,000 years ago. It's the verse from 1 Thessalonians shown above.

See, even back then, wise leaders knew about differentiated practice—that we need to adjust our leadership to the individual and to his/her situation. And a lot of the variation in our response is based upon our assessment of people on two dimensions: their *will* and their *skill* to do good work. For example, some folks have the skills needed. They know what to do but, perhaps because doing good work requires a great deal of diligence and dedicated effort, choose not to bring those skills consistently to bear. For those "idle" souls, correction (i.e., admonishment) is needed. Others have the skills and interest in doing good work but lack the confidence (i.e., are fainthearted). For such individuals, our main work is to build up belief in themselves so their light can shine. Still, for another group of people, a lack of skills needed for the job make them "weak." Of course, the major work here is to help such individuals learn about and develop the key skills that will make them effective contributors to the group.

Underlying the simple wisdom of this passage is the idea that I, as leader, can discern what each person needs: admonishment, encouragement, or help. Then, when I can perceive what is truly required, that I can and will deliver what is needed, faithfully and effectively.

Perhaps that is why the closing message in Paul's counsel is to "be patient with them all." And *all* means you, too, as such skills will take time—perhaps even a lifetime—to develop. But with God's guidance and your faith in Him, you can figure this out. "It" is in you if He is in you— guiding you and your leadership of others. Trust that and be patient with that, so you may be patient, understanding, and effective with every sort of soul under your charge.

Dear Lord,

Thank You for the opportunity to lead Your children. Guide my steps through Your wisdom and understanding. Strengthen my resolve to do what is needed and to be at peace with the results.

Into Your Loving Hands, I place my trust and faith.

Amen.

25

OFFERING FORGIVENESS

"Jesus said, 'Father, forgive them, for they do not know what they are doing.'"

(Luke 23:34)

"Christ, you know it ain't easy
You know how hard it can be
The way things are going
They're going to crucify me."

S o goes the chorus of the John Lennon classic, "The Ballad of John and Yoko."

It's a lyric that resonates at some point with just about anyone, because there will come that time when it seems the forces in one's world are conspiring against her. In response, a person needs to have the courage of her convictions — that moment of undeniable clarity when she knows she *must* do what she does not *want* to do — for doing what is needed will likely incur great personal cost, seemingly all she has.

Understandably, such a moment can be extremely taxing and visible and lonely. But it can also be a time of sublime grace, as we perhaps connect with Our Savior and His cross for the first time in any visceral way and as we come to understand — maybe for the first time — what it really means to "have *our own cross* to bear."

At times such as these, we are wise to follow the age-old counsel to "take up your cross and follow Christ." And, in particular, to *follow* Christ's story and Christ's example of how He perceived and bore His cross in order to gain guidance and support in bearing our own.

For example, from the passion of Christ we come to understand:

That not everything is fair or just;

That betrayal perhaps hurts the most;

That leaders and their motives are often misunderstood;

That ignorance prevails more oft' than it should;

That we are asked to take on more than we feel we can bear;

That despite all this, our Lord is there!

Yes, we can (and we should) take great comfort in knowing we have a God who **does understand** how it feels—that we are not alone. In fact, we probably are never more supported or "carried" than in times such as these. So, yes, John Lennon, **Christ does know "it ain't easy,"** and, yes, **Christ does know "how hard it can be."** That's why Christ's example of humbly embracing a cross He did not earn, yet amazingly accepted with a loving, merciful, and forgiving heart, is even more convicting to those who strive to tread His path. The sublime strength of will and humility of heart to express, amid great personal suffering, "Father, forgive them, for they do not know what they are doing" is something to truly amaze, marvel, and deeply ponder ...

Do we possess comparable strength of soul to raise a similar prayer from our forgiving hearts for those associated with the crosses we must bear in this world?

For perhaps our biggest takeaway from Christ's example is that it never really was about the suffering or the injustice or the misunderstandings, anyway. It seems those are all just part of the human condition on this planet. No, the major understanding that we need to derive from even our most challenging moments is this: that when all is said and done, **love and mercy and <u>forgiveness</u> prevail.**

Dear Lord,

It is so easy to play the role of victim and overlook my own contributions to the problems at hand in my life and in this world. Please help me to see with Your eyes and take steps down Your path, so that, even in my most severe of trials, I can see those around me not so much as adversaries but rightly as Your Children and My Brothers and Sisters. Despite our differences or offenses—real or perceived—please help me to cultivate a forgiving, merciful, and loving heart so I may live ever more in peace and joy, and so that You may increasingly use me as an instrument of Your ongoing love letter to the world.

In Your Mighty Name, I pray.

Amen.

26

REMAINING STRONG
AND TRUE

"Have I not commanded you?
Be strong and courageous. Do not be frightened,
and do not be dismayed, for the Lord your God
is with you wherever you go."

(Joshua 1:9)

Years ago, during the first few days of my very first job as a school leader, a trusted colleague told me something that I carry to this day: "Being a school leader is probably the world's best ongoing values clarification exercise." How right he was! As I got to know the people in my new school community, wade into the issues that accompanied their lives, and ultimately made decisions in line with my responsibilities, I had to sort out what I believed was right and just in a world with few "black and white" markers. Through the process of weighing out the complex problems of human life and making my decisions, I was essentially revealing, testing, and shaping my core beliefs; and given my formal leadership role in the school, I was thus, over time, also simultaneously revealing, testing, and shaping the values of my school community. The world's best ongoing values clarification exercise, indeed!

Over time, I came to deeply appreciate the way the leader's decision-making responsibilities helped me figure out who I am and what I believe in terms of core values. But making decisions in accord with principles of what one can best discern is right and just is often not popular whatsoever. At such times, the leadership journey seems trod on a deserted path. Yet in such forlorn hours, we are always accompanied by our truest friend, as William Barclay perhaps says best, "There are certain decisions which must be taken and certain roads that must be walked in the awful loneliness of our own souls. And yet, in the deepest sense of all, even in these times, we are not alone, for never is God nearer to us."

Yes, the leadership journey can certainly seem lonely at times. But take great heart, for **one of the most sublime of gifts arising from a lifetime of service is an abiding clarity—that we are never LESS alone than when we are doing His work for His children, helping as many as we can to find their fruitful path.**

> *"Nothing before, nothing behind*
> *The steps of faith*
> *Fall on the seeming void, and find*
> *The rock beneath."*

(John Greenleaf Whittier)

Dear Lord,

Thank you for the road that you have prepared especially for me. Knowing that You always go before me and are with me, let me always move with confidence and courage down that path, regardless of what may arise along the journey. I pray that You guide me in my steps and that I may be open to Your guidance so I may remain strong and true until that glorious day when I finally arrive home with You.

Amen.

BIBLIOGRAPHY

Barclay, W. (2001). *The gospel of mark.* Edinburgh, Saint Andrew Press.

Barth, R. S. (2003). *Lessons learned: Shaping relationships and the culture of the workplace.* Thousand Oaks, CA: Corwin.

Bolman, L.G., & Deal, T. E. (1995). *Leading with soul: An uncommon journey of spirit.* San Francisco, CA: Jossey-Bass.

Collins, J. (2001). *Good to great: Why some companies make the leap and others don't.* New York, NY: HarperCollins.

Deal, T.E., & Peterson, K. D. (2003). *Shaping school culture: The heart of leadership.* San Francisco, CA: Jossey-Bass.

DuVernay, A. (2015). *Selma.* Retrieved from http://www.imdb.com/title/tt1020072

Gandhi, M. K., & Gandhi, M. K. (1993). *Gandhi: An autobiography – the story of my experiments with truth.* Boston, MA: Beacon Press.

Kolodiejchuk, B. (2007). *Mother teresa: Come be my light*. New York, NY: Doubleday.

Kouzes, J.M., & Posner, B.Z. (1993). *Credibility: How leaders gain and lose it, why people demand it*. San Francisco, CA: Jossey-Bass.

Lewis, C. S. (2015). *Mere christianity*. New York, NY: HarperCollins.

Life application study bible, new international version. (1983). Carol Stream, IL: Tyndale.

Mandela, N. (1995). *Long walk to freedom: The autobiography of nelson mandela*. New York, NY: Back Bay Books.

McPherson, J. M. (1988). *Battle cry of freedom: The civil war era*. Oxford: Oxford University Press.

McPherson, J.M. (2003). *Hallowed ground: A walk at gettysburg*. New York, NY: Crown Publishers.

Miller, S. J. (2004). *D. L. moody on spiritual leadership*. Chicago, IL: Moody Publishers.

Nouwen, H. J. M. (1972). *With open hands*. Notre Dame, IN: Ave Maria Press.

Oates, S. B. (1977). *With malice toward none: A life of abraham lincoln*. New York, NY: Harper & Row.

Rohr. R. (2017). *Richard rohr's daily meditation.* Retrieved from https://cac.org/category/daily- meditations.

Rohr, R. (2015). *What the mystics know: Seven pathways to your deeper self.* New York, NY: Crossroad Publishing.

Thoreau, H. D. (1983). *Walden and civil disobedience.* New York, NY: Penguin Books.

Vardey, L. (1995). *Mother teresa: A simple path.* New York, NY: Ballantine Books.

Wilkinson, B. (2005). *Beyond jabez: expanding your borders.* Sisters, OR: Multnomah Publishers.

Wooden, J. (2003). *They call me coach.* New York, NY: McGraw-Hill.

ABOUT THE AUTHOR

D r. Joe Schroeder is a Wisconsin native who was raised to value hard work, education, and fair dealing. Through God's Almighty grace and providence, the joys and trials of Joe's personal and professional life deepened his faith in immeasurable and unforeseen ways, which ultimately prompted this book.

A love of learning and a deep-seated desire to positively impact others spurred Joe to pursue his secondary education-English teaching degree, as well as two graduate degrees in educational administration from the University of Wisconsin (BS, 1988; MS, 1995; PhD, 2001). Joe is entering his 30th year in education, having served in a variety of roles, including high school teacher and coach, principal, director of instruction, superintendent, and university instructor. Joe currently serves as the associate executive director for the Association of Wisconsin School Administrators (AWSA), where he is blessed to facilitate the learning of educators at every level of leadership, while he learns alongside them.

Since raising their three daughters, Joe and his wife, Annie, continue a multi-year renovation of their small farmstead in Delafield, Wisconsin, that is filled with all sorts of critters and which provides virtually endless opportunities for functional fitness, as well as abundant ongoing humility training.

Joe can be reached at joes2326@gmail.com or via Twitter @joeschroeder23

Made in the USA
Monee, IL
16 October 2020